"The routes outlined here are explore everything there is to o to perhaps achieve that blissful s ... ulfilment."

A few years ago when I was walking the Herriot Way in the Yorkshire Dales with some friends we stopped in the King's Arms in Askrigg, having already walked 13 miles of an 18-mile day. As I sat on the bench in the cosy little back room of the bar and took a refreshing draught of my pint of Black Sheep I drifted off into something of a reverie.

The scenery had been beautiful all day despite a bit of drizzle, the company couldn't have been better, and the pub and beer whisked me into a different world. I was aware of everything around me, but I was also blissfully happy in an almost thoughtless state.

Walking can do that to us sometimes – maybe it's that sense of having earned our reward? Whatever the trigger, it's a priceless feeling and one that I have happily experienced on many other occasions in some of the excellent hostelries featured in these pages.

Seeking nirvana

The routes outlined here are designed to help you explore everything there is to offer in the region and to perhaps achieve that blissful sense of fulfilment. There's a full range of length and difficulty, from the mile and half or so around Ryhall and Belmesthorpe and a lovely two-mile stroll in Ketton, to the much longer routes in the Chater and Welland valleys.

We have a wonderful area on our doorstep and all the walks are superb in their own way, whether that's because of pretty valleys, gurgling streams, enchanting country lanes, thatched roofs or magnificent churches. If you happen to include a pitstop at any of the hostelries along the way, you may also ascend to the aforementioned state of nirvana. Although I suspect it's something which cannot be achieved on demand - sometimes it's there and sometimes it's not. Either way, you will have a cracking walk and the chance to support a local business and thoroughly enjoy your well-deserved time away from the daily grind.

On the subject of local businesses, in 2019 I attended a magical wedding at Molecey Mill between West Deeping and Market Deeping, and we were delighted to collaborate with the dynamic team there to bring you this book. You can read more about Molecey Mill on pages 36-37.

In dispatches

We haven't got the space to mention all the great pubs in the area and there are some which have featured in previous books that we just couldn't squeeze into this one, but you can always visit them another time.

Also, it's worth me mentioning we haven't partnered with any of the pubs included in these pages. They are all here because we like them, and they make for a good place to rest those weary legs. There are some words of advice about enjoying the area in a safe and responsible manner at the back of the book but, above all, my recommendation is to get out there and explore.

Caveat: there's never been a more difficult time in the hospitality industry, and we can't guarantee how long all the wonderful places mentioned in this book will be run by the same people or will even be open. Therefore, my only advice is, use them or lose them.

Happy walking!

Will Hetherington

First published in the United Kingdom in 2024 by Triangle Publishing Ltd Eventus Business Centre Sunderland Road Market Deeping PE6 8FD

ISBN 978-1-8382124-4-5

This book can be ordered from the publisher at **www.theactivemag.com** or try your local bookshop.

We have taken every care to ensure these walks are up-to-date and accurate at the time of publication. If you notice any changes or errors, please let us know by email to **walks@theactivemag.com** We will endeavour to update the information for the next printing of the book.

The maps in this guide are for illustration only and you should take your own OS map or a navigation device on all walks.

Author
Will Hetherington

Design
Matt Tarrant

Publishers
Triangle Publishing Ltd

Foreword

Walking is good for you both physically and mentally and costs absolutely nothing; so many positives in those few words. And because it costs you nothing it means you might just have a bit of cash left in your pocket to enjoy a well-deserved drink or meal in one of our favourite hostelries in the area after a good leg stretch.

In my opinion a good walk is best rounded off with a sit down and a cup of tea or glass of something cheerful. You can then enjoy resting your legs after your efforts and contemplate where you have just been and what, or who, you may have encountered on the way. And all in pleasant, welcoming surroundings; what's not to like? I have my favourite, regular spots but am very grateful that Will has come up with this great idea for our fourth book; he's combined fabulous walks with some of his favourite pubs which are the perfect pairing.

You can have a short stroll of a couple of miles and end up in the pub afterwards or tackle a longer ramble and enjoy much needed sustenance at the end of it, and justify a pudding as well. Will has been out doing his research and has come up with excellent routes and pubs to suit all of us, so there really is something for everyone who wants to enjoy a walk in this book.

We all know that pubs have had a particularly hard time in the last few years so if we want to see them survive and thrive we need to support them. Most, or all, of them serve tea and coffee so cater for everyone. And if they have a roaring open fire or log burner going in the winter that's me settled for the duration.

It's been a great pleasure to team up with **Molecey Mill** to bring you this new book, and thank you to every one of you who has bought a copy. Enjoy the walks and the pubs. And who knows you may pop into one and find Will sitting in the corner contemplating life, and I might well be with him doing the same.

Mary Bremner - Editor, Active Magazine

Mr MOLECEY'S
Marvellous Mill

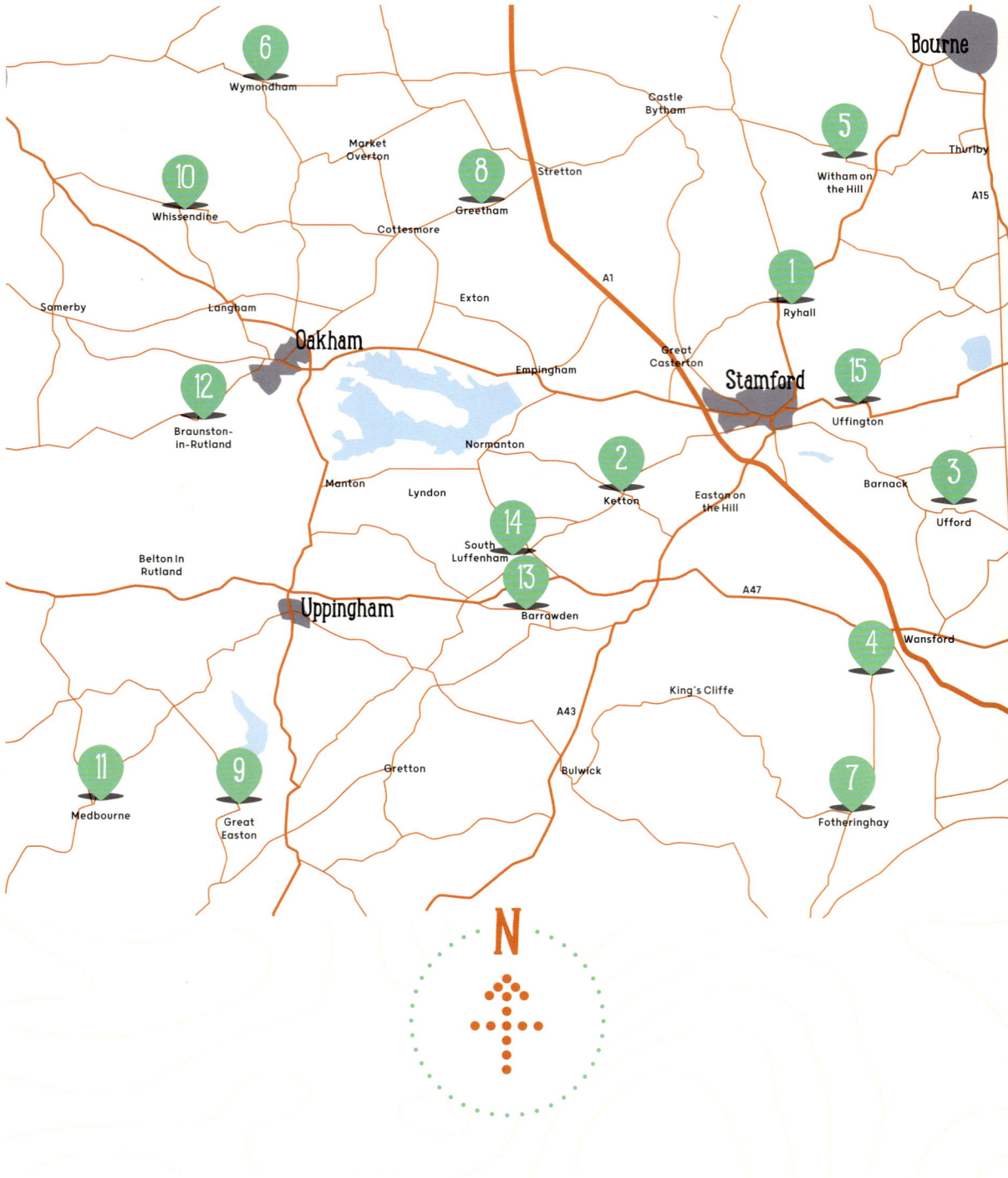

Bourne

6 — Wymondham

5 — Witham on the Hill

Thurlby

Castle Bytham

Market Overton

10 — Whissendine

8 — Greetham

Stretton

A15

Cottesmore

A1

1 — Ryhall

Somerby

Langham

Exton

Great Casterton

Oakham

Empingham

Stamford

15 — Uffington

12 — Braunston-in-Rutland

Normanton

Barnack

3 — Ufford

Manton

Lyndon

2 — Ketton

Easton on the Hill

Belton In Rutland

14 — South Luffenham

A47

Uppingham

13 — Barrowden

4 — Wansford

King's Cliffe

11 — Medbourne

9 — Great Easton

Gretton

A43

Bulwick

7 — Fotheringhay

N

The walks

ROUTE MAP KEY

S/F Start/finish   Walk route   ◀ Direction   ◯ Village / Town   Woodland

Road   River/lake/reservoir   Railway   ✝ Church   PH Public House

1. Ryhall and Belmesthorpe

This very short stroll is a bit more accessible than most of the other walks in the book and links two lovely villages with some handy pubs.

THE ROUTE

Park near the village hall in Ryhall and head east down the path by the side of the primary school. Keeping the line of trees on your right you will soon come to the playground which may come in handy if you have the children with you.

Walk through the playground and go through the gate beyond. Turn left here to walk around the perimeter of the large grazing field. The right-hand side is often temporarily fenced off for sheep, but the left-hand side is usually accessible. When you take this option you will have the River Gwash on your left for most of the way around the field with a good access point for dogs along the way.

On the far side of the field you will find another gate through to a smaller field. Keep going and you will get to the footbridge over the Gwash. Once you have crossed the bridge turn right to make a short detour up to the Blue Bell, a pub which has seen a welcome transformation recently with plenty of room outdoors and indoors for people popping in as part of a country stroll.

To resume the route simply walk back down the hill, passing the lovely bench overlooking the Gwash on the way. This is a great place for the dog to have a paddle and to enjoy the peaceful view of this lovely little river. Once you have passed the footbridge stay on the road as it bends its way towards Ryhall. It's a quiet country road and is never particularly busy, so it makes a nice part of the walk.

You will come into Ryhall and, after some newer houses, you will start to see some older stone cottages on both sides of the road. Keep going and you will soon come to the pretty bridge with white railings back over the Gwash which carries a single lane for motorised traffic. Turn left and cross the bridge and you will find the Green Dragon pub in the village centre. To get back to the car you can walk round on the road or take the little path which goes up the side of the Green Dragon and through the churchyard.

LOCAL KNOWLEDGE

If you don't mind a bit more of a detour then go and see the llamas on the south side of Belmesthorpe. Head up to Castle Rise by taking a right and a left after the pub and look out for the footpath between two houses. This leads up to the llama fields, with some pigs and rare breed sheep beyond.

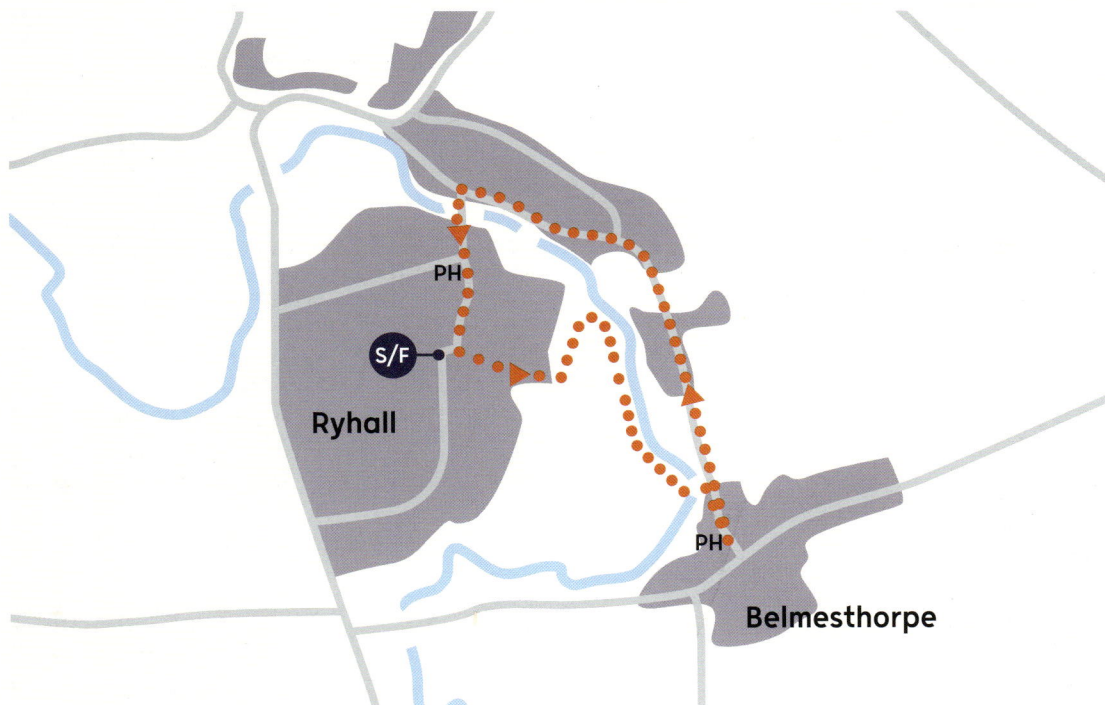

PH

S/F

Ryhall

PH

Belmesthorpe

ESSENTIAL INFORMATION

Difficulty rating

One paw. It's a short walk with no stiles and is flat. More than half is on tarmac.

Where to park
Near the village hall in Ryhall.

Distance
One and half miles.

Highlights
A lovely meadow linking the two villages, Ryhall church, some good pubs and views of the pretty little river Gwash.

Refreshments
The Blue Bell in Belmesthorpe and the Green Dragon in Ryhall.

The pooch perspective
It's a short walk but there are some easy places for your dog to get into the river. There may be sheep.

2. Ketton, Aldgate and Geeston

A short walk with some gorgeous stone houses, a section of bucolic countryside and a fine pub to slake your thirst.

THE ROUTE

Start on spectacular Church Road and walk up Chapel Lane to the left of the pub. When you reach the end turn right on to Redmile's Lane and stay on the path into Hall Close play area. Walk over the grass until you reach Bull Lane at the far end. Turn right here and cross the Chater. I have stopped on the bench here for something to eat and drink on many a long walk and there are few nicer spots to stop for a while.

After the bench take the left turn and go through the gate into a narrow channel which then opens out into the sheep pastures on the south side of the Chater. Keep going through the grassy fields, with the river on your left, until you reach the farm track at the end. Turn right here and stay on the track up a slight hill and then down the other side towards the railway bridge. Go under the bridge and turn right immediately. Follow the path in a straight line, passing the sewage works on your left, until you come to the north eastern end of Geeston Road.

You will very shortly come to a footpath sign on the right signposted Aldgate. Take this path which leads back over the railway on a pedestrian bridge and into Aldgate. When you reach Edmond's Drive keep going straight ahead and you will see the path tucked behind some bushes. Follow the path and you will come out on the south side of the two bridges (road and pedestrian) over the Chater in the middle of the village.

Walk over the bridge, past the magnificent church and right back to the Railway Inn, one of the most popular pubs in the area and an absolute goldmine if you happen to like well-kept real ale. Don't just take my word for it. The Railway was awarded the 2024 Campaign for Real Ale (CAMRA) Pub of the Year across the whole of the Leicestershire, Northamptonshire and Rutland region, to go with its Pub of the Year Award from Rutland CAMRA.

Ketton   PH   Aldgate
S/F

LOCAL KNOWLEDGE

In August 1928 Ketton Portland Cement Company was incorporated and construction of a cement works began. It was producing cement within a year and, by the end of 1929, the 140 men and two women on the permanent payroll had produced and despatched 8,500 tonnes of cement. The limestone and clay needed for cement production is supplied by Grange Top quarry and the site continues to be one of the most efficient cement producers in Europe.

ESSENTIAL INFORMATION

Difficulty rating

🐾 🐾 🐾 🐾 🐾

One paw. It's a short walk with no stiles and is generally good underfoot.

Where to park
The walk starts near the Railway Inn so as close as you can to the pub.

Distance
Two miles.

Highlights
A beautiful church and some stunning old houses around the pretty bridges at the bottom of Church Road. A peaceful bench looking over the Chater in Aldgate. A deservedly popular pub.

Refreshments
The multi-award-winning Railway Inn. There is also the Rutland Vineyard just to the west of the village on Barrowden Road.

The pooch perspective
You probably won't exhaust a fit dog on this route, but there's a couple of good spots to get in the river. There will also be sheep on the south side of the Chater after you leave Aldgate.

3. Ufford and Ashton

Taking in part of the Torpel Way this route makes for a perfect evening stroll.

THE ROUTE

Park in Ufford somewhere near the White Hart pub and walk south down the main road. After you pass magnificent Ufford Hall on the left you will see a footpath sign at Ufford Farm pointing to the right. Take this turn and walk down the picturesque lane. Stay on the lane for about five minutes but approximately 50 metres before it opens out into the field ahead take the quick left/right turn to walk along the northern side of the hedge. There is a post in the end of the hedge but it's quite overgrown and not obvious.

Once you have switched to this side of the hedge keep heading east for a kilometre, passing The Jubilee wood on the right before you reach the road.

At the road turn left and follow the tarmac north for about 600 metres. It's such a quiet country lane I would be surprised if you see one car. You will walk into monastically quiet Ashton with Gamekeeper's Cottage on your right.

Turn left at the junction in the village and when the road bends to the right you will see the footpath heading straight on. Take this path and you are now on the Torpel Way (which links Stamford and Peterborough) for a stretch. Follow the path through a grass field and then out into the arable fields until you reach the next road.

Cross the road and go over the pretty wooden pedestrian bridge, and carry on until you reach the next field boundary, where there is a low bench. Turn left here and leave the Torpel Way to wend its way towards Stamford. Follow the path across one field and then along the side of two more, passing over a small stream along the way, which might be useful for the dog in hot weather.

When you reach the road, turn right and follow it all the way back into Ufford. When you get back to the village it's well worth a quick detour up to the church where there are some nice countryside views from the elevated position. After that the White Hart beckons.

> ❝
> **You will walk into Monastically quiet Ashton with Gamekeeper's Cottage on your right.**

LOCAL KNOWLEDGE

The Torpel Way covers approximately 12 miles from Peterborough to Stamford, passing Marholm, Helpston, Ashton and Barnack before finishing with a riverside stretch along the Welland into Stamford. It's a peaceful route dominated by low rolling countryside and arable farming.

Bainton

Ashton

Ufford

PH

S/F

ESSENTIAL INFORMATION

Difficulty rating

One paw; there's nothing tricky here with no stiles and generally firm underfoot conditions.

Where to park
Somewhere near the White Hart pub in Ufford.

Distance
Three miles (although you can easily extend this by including Barnack in your loop if you want a longer route).

Highlights
Undisturbed Ashton sees almost no through traffic and has an old-fashioned peace as a result. The church in Ufford occupies an elevated position and provides great views.

Refreshments
The White Hart at Ufford.

The pooch perspective
It's more of a gentle stroll than an epic adventure but your dog will get a decent walk. There's not normally any livestock because this is arable land and there is one stream near the end.

4. Yarwell and Nassington

These two villages are linked by the Nene Way as it follows the river from Oundle to Peterborough.

THE ROUTE

Park somewhere near the Angel in Yarwell and walk east along the road, passing the church on the right as you go. Follow the road round to the right and look out for the path on the left clearly signposted for the Nene Way Footpath and the Nene Valley Railway. Head down here and take the right turn in less than a minute where there is a marker on the post. Keep heading south, past the alpacas on your right, until you come to the access road to Yarwell Mill. Turn left here to walk downhill into the holiday complex.

When you get to the old mill turn right and then turn right again immediately to pass the café and cross the bridge over the lock.

Keep following the Nene Way signs and a few minutes after the lock you will come to a sign to the Nene Valley Railway to the left where there is a bridge. It is probably worth a little detour to the NVR station if you have time, but it will add another half a mile or so to the walk.

> **"**
> It is probably worth a little
> detour to the NVR station if you
> have time, but it will add another
> half a mile or so to the walk."

Ms
MOLECEY'S
Marvellous Mill

LOCAL KNOWLEDGE

Described as a hidden gem and King Cnut's Royal Manor, the Prebendal Manor in Nassington dates from the early 13th century, and is the oldest dwelling in Northamptonshire.

If you don't go to the railway then carry straight on at the bridge. There are some excellent places around here for dogs to get into the river if they need to cool off and have a drink. With the Nene tributary on your left, after a while you will start to arc southwest across the flood plain towards Nassington. There is another bridge over the Nene along the way, with grand views of the river in both directions.

Ancient buildings

When you reach the village turn right and then first left on to Church Street. At the top of the gentle incline, you will find the ancient Prebendal Abbey on the left and the church to the right. You can walk through the churchyard and then keep heading north on Church Street and carry straight on to Northfield Lane where the main road bends to the left. Keep going past Lily Pad Cottages on your left and you will come to the bridleway and the ford almost as soon as you leave the village.

Pass under the old railway bridge and stay on the track in a straight line for half a mile until you reach Nassington Road. Turn left here and walk along the pavement alongside the road towards Yarwell for a minute or two. Just as you reach the village there is a footpath to the right across the playing fields. Take this path and then the first left to bring you back to the Angel Inn.

"

There are some excellent places around here for dogs to get into the river if they need to cool off and have a drink."

ESSENTIAL INFORMATION

Difficulty rating

🐾 🐾 🐾 🐾 🐾

One paw; there's nothing tricky here, except the bridleway back to Yarwell can get a bit muddy.

Where to park
Near the Angel Inn in Yarwell.

Distance
Three and a quarter miles but if you want an even shorter route you can just walk to Wansford and back from Yarwell.

Highlights
The impressive Nene meandering through the floodplain. Yarwell Mill and lock. Nassington church and the Prebendal Manor.

Refreshments
The Angel Inn at Yarwell and there is a small café down by Yarwell Mill.

The pooch perspective
Your dogs will love this walk. They can cool off down by the Nene and they can enjoy the bridleway back to Yarwell.

5. Witham on the Hill

This walk is just the right distance to blow the cobwebs away and work up an appetite.

THE ROUTE

I tend to park on the road by St Andrew's church, but you can park anywhere in the village. Take the footpath which runs down the left side of the church, go through the gate and head down the hill. Turn left just before the bridge over the stream and then follow the path to the gateway. Turn right here and walk straight up the road and out of the village, gradually climbing as you go. The path here is a well-established roadway so it's pretty easy going.

You will continue with some woodland on your left and an open field on the right. When you come to the thin belt of woodland on your right-hand side you will see the path heading off to the right before the next gateway. Take this path through the trees and you will soon come to a footpath junction with a signpost. Take the left-hand option and you very shortly come out into a large open field with views out towards Toft. Turn left and follow the path with the hedge on your left all the way down to the end of the field. Here you will see the gateway leading to a bridge over the East Glen river.

Country lanes…

Cross the bridge and carry on to the road up towards the tiny hamlet of Lound. Walk up the hill to the road junction and turn right towards Toft. This tree-lined country lane between Toft and Lound is extremely quiet and, as roads go, it's a pleasure to walk on. After about half a mile you will walk around a left-hand bend and you will see the Toft House Hotel immediately on your right. Turn right here and head out of Toft, staying on the right side of the main road with the golf course to your left on the other side of the road.

Take care when walking over the narrow humpback bridge with cars coming into the village at some speed. It's best to wait until there are no cars approaching before nipping over, and then almost immediately afterwards take the footpath which veers off to the right and over the fields and up the hill.

The first section is clearly marked but after you cross the second stile, the path carries on into the field for 100 metres or so and then there is a left turn. This brings you to an access road where you turn right and on the outskirts of the village you will pass a large modern house on your left called Witham Grange. Take the left turn shortly afterwards to join a footpath which crosses the stream and then takes you back up to the church.

If you want to enjoy a good meal afterwards then book a table for lunch or dinner at the Six Bells in Witham.

> **66**
>
> This tree-lined country lane between Toft and Lound is extremely quiet and, as roads go, it's a pleasure to walk on."

LOCAL KNOWLEDGE

The little-known Toft railway tunnel on the Eastern & Midlands railway line is to the north of the village and was completed in 1893. It connected the industrial midlands with the east coast ports and saw its last trains on February 28, 1959.

Lound

Toft

Witham on the Hill

PH

S/F

Manthorpe

ESSENTIAL INFORMATION

Difficulty rating

🐾🐾🐾⬜⬜

Three paws. Not too challenging but there are a few contours and the uphill climb on the return to Witham might be a bit heavy underfoot. Plus there are some tricky stiles.

Where to park
Either on the road near the church or somewhere else in the village.

Distance
Four miles.

Highlights
A decent combination of contours means you will be well exercised but not exhausted. Witham is an attractive village with an excellent pub/ restaurant.

Refreshments
The Six Bells in Witham has one of the best reputations in the area largely as a restaurant, but you can pop in for a drink too.

The pooch perspective
You will probably see a few sheep on the way round. The dogs can get into the East Glen river at Toft and just before Lound.

Mr
MOLECEY'S
Marvellous Mill

6. Wymondham and Edmondthorpe

Fine views from the top of Cord Hill, two very different rural communities, and a thriving pub make this route one to remember.

THE ROUTE

Park in Wymondham on Main Street near the Old Bakery Antiques shop and Spring Lane. Walk south down Spring Lane and follow the path out of the village, passing the gorgeous Old Rectory on the right. Almost immediately you will pass through Spring Farm. Bear right after the main farmhouse on to a path with some woodland on your right, until you come to a footpath junction. Turn left into a narrow grassy field. Walk to the bottom of this field, turn left, cross the footbridge and then almost immediately turn right and right again after the gate to pick up the footpath to Cord Hill. (There are a few inter-linked footpaths around the southern half of the village but there is only one path up to Cord Hill).

Once you are on the right track it's the best part of a mile to the hill, but the path is obvious. Some sections of it are on grass and others are on farm access roads. The 'private' signs on either side will keep you on the right track too.

LOCAL KNOWLEDGE

The stable buildings at the now ruined Edmondthorpe Hall were used to house Italian and then German prisoners of war in the Second World War.

Even though it's not particularly steep or high, the panoramic views from the top of Cord Hill are surprisingly good. With Whissendine Station and Stapleford Park Hotel in the immediate vicinity and plenty more further afield, it's worth stopping to enjoy the view for a while. When you have had your fill of the scenery, make a sharp left turn immediately after you go through the gap in the hedge at the top, to then follow the path as it gradually drops down along the edge of the field. When you reach the tarmac road, turn left and follow the road for approximately one mile. It's a lovely leafy lane, and you won't see many vehicles as it winds its way to the junction with Edmondthorpe Road.

When you get to the junction head straight on and walk into the attractive little old estate village of Edmondthorpe, which is on a dead-end road and is always as quiet as a Sunday morning. Stay on the road and pass the pretty little church on your right. After about 150 yards take the footpath off to the left. Bear right at the first junction and then keep heading north back towards Wymondham. Just before the path reaches the road outside Wymondham turn left and cross the stream.

Keep going and cross the main road into the village to walk on to Nurses Lane and follow it round past the church and back to the centre of this bustling rural community. If you have timed it right and booked ahead, you can go for lunch or dinner in the Berkeley Arms and round off the walk in style. Alternatively, you can head up to Wymondham Windmill Tearooms which are based around the 200-year-old windmill which has been partially restored.

Wymondham

Edmondthorpe

ESSENTIAL INFORMATION

Difficulty rating

🐾🐾⬜⬜⬜

Two paws; there's nothing tricky here.

Where to park
On Main Street in Wymondham near the Old Bakery Antiques shop and Spring Lane.

Distance
Four and a quarter miles.

Highlights
Panoramic views from the top of Cord Hill, remote and peaceful little Edmondthorpe, Wymondham Windmill and the excellent Berkeley Arms.

Refreshments
The Berkeley Arms and Wymondham Windmill Tearooms. Or the Black Bull in nearby Market Overton.

The pooch perspective
There's quite an extensive ground nesting bird programme here, so you need to keep the dogs under control, but they will still enjoy it with some stream access along the way. Very little livestock.

Ms MOLECEY'S
Marvellous Mill

7. Fotheringhay and Elton

With bags of history and plenty of pretty scenery this loop is perfect for a Sunday stroll.

THE ROUTE

This classic Sunday afternoon route features one of the most significant churches in the whole area, two beautiful villages, the mighty river Nene and as much history as you could possibly want. You can start in either Elton or Fotheringhay, and for this guide I will start in the latter. This impressive settlement makes a splendid start and finish point, with its octagonal-towered church, sweeping main street, grand houses and impossible-to-ignore connection to Mary Queen of Scots. If you didn't know, Mary was executed at the castle here on 8 February 1587, aged 44, after years of imprisonment at various sites around England.

Start the walk at the church gates and head south east along the main road. When you get to the big right-hand turn in the road pick up the Nene Way footpath straight ahead.

After passing through a farm, you will find the old site of the motte and bailey castle on your right. As the site of the execution in February 1587 it's an integral part of British history and an interesting staging post on the walk. After the castle stay on the Nene Way and keep heading south east up and over a gentle undulation, through some arable crops, and you will eventually come to a sheep pasture, followed by a lock on the river Nene. Cross the river and continue along the Nene Way. You will see plenty of long boats ahead moored up on a side-water and the path then goes through the old Warmington Mill.

Immediately after the mill, make sure you take the left turn before the Nene Way goes underneath the A605. From here the footpath runs alongside a raised section of the main road for 400 yards but it's totally segregated so feels both safe and reasonably quiet. You soon come to a left turn which leads to a track that traverses a bank above a long strip of woodland heading north, with poly-tunnels on the right. Stay on the track and you will eventually come to a gateway which leads straight into the southern section of Elton Park. The path goes through the park and offers some splendid views as you approach the village, which you will enter on Chapel Lane.

Elton and beyond

Turn left and make sure you take the next footpath to the left leading directly off Stocks Green (unless you are making a worthwhile detour to The Crown just around the corner). You will know you are on the right path because it very quickly takes you past the mill and then the majestic river Nene as it sweeps through the Northamptonshire countryside. Cross the river and turn right immediately. There is a good spot here for the dogs to get into the river. Carry on over the smaller footbridge and turn left immediately.

Head west out over the flat field and when you get to the dismantled railway, take the path which runs south west towards Middle Lodge and is very clearly marked through the field. After two fields you will come to Middle Lodge, an isolated farmstead. Take the left-hand route all around the farm buildings and pick up the path again on the other side. After another two fields you will reach Fotheringhay Road just 500 yards north of the village. Walk down the road enjoying the impressive view of the church and then reward yourself with a trip to the Falcon.

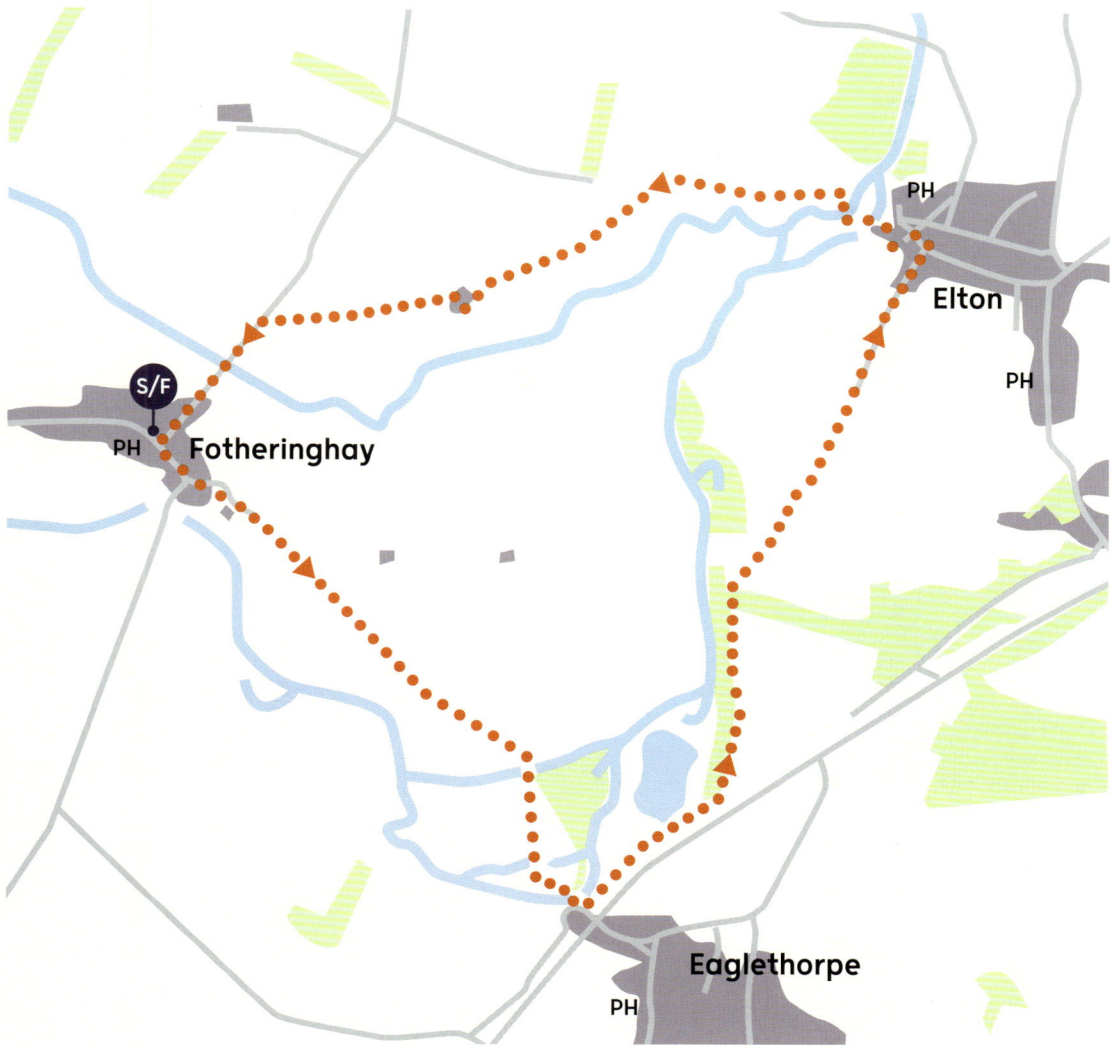

S/F

PH **Fotheringhay**

PH **Elton**

PH

Eaglethorpe

PH

ESSENTIAL INFORMATION

Difficulty rating

🐾🐾⚪⚪⚪

Two paws; it might be five miles but it's good underfoot and there aren't many contours.

Where to park
On the main road in Fotheringhay near the church.

Distance
Five miles.

Highlights
Three lovely pubs and villages, Fotheringhay church and castle, the river Nene, and the beautiful English countryside.

Refreshments
The Crown and the Black Horse in Elton and the Falcon in Fotheringhay.

The pooch perspective
A couple of good cooling off spots in the Nene, largely arable but there might be some livestock

8. Greetham and Fort Henry

A walk in open country on largely good tracks, including a rare straight mile, with the enchanting Fort Henry thrown in for good measure.

THE ROUTE

Park where you can in Greetham and set off on the Viking Way which runs south off the main road through the village, almost opposite Great Lane. You will soon pass a couple of chicken farms on either side of the track. After about one kilometre the path takes a right/left around the corner of a small piece of woodland, after which you will be on an estate road. Keep heading south, ignoring the signposted left hand turn on to a farm track lined with small trees. You will then walk down into a dip and up the other side.

Once you are heading east after the dip, ignore the path to the right running down the western edge of Tunnelly Wood (unless you want to make a detour into beautiful Exton), and enjoy the next mile of dead straight walking on a very well-maintained access road. In most cases you will have the whole road to yourself, apart from the occasional dog walker, or farm vehicle. It's very peaceful (apart from the Great North Road in the far distance which you won't hear even with an easterly wind), and a great chance to stride out on an enjoyable dead straight mile – a rare occurrence indeed.

When you reach the end of the straight track you will see Lower Lake to your right and then Fort Henry Lake to your left, with the eponymous boathouse on its west shore. Take the left hand turn off the track at the signpost and you will lose sight of the lake behind the wood for a minute or two. But at the northern edge of the wood, you get an even better view of the boathouse.

A choice of return routes

After that, follow the winding track alongside the North Brook on boggy ground until you reach the embankment. Go up the steps and then you have a choice. You can either drop down the other side and follow the winding path through the golf course and then past Brook Farm back into Greetham on Wheatsheaf Lane.

Or you can turn left and walk along the farm track for one mile until you reach the right hand turn at the lone mature tree, and then follow the path north all the way back into Greetham, where it joins Wheatsheaf Lane just before the Wheatsheaf pub.

They are both good options, although the second does involve some quite boggy fields. On balance the golf course route is probably more interesting, and better underfoot in the wetter months of the year.

LOCAL KNOWLEDGE

The battle of Losecoat Field took place to the east of Fort Henry in 1470. Lincolnshire nobleman Robert Welles, whose father was held prisoner by King Edward IV, assembled a force to rebel against the King, who marched an army to meet the rebels. The King then had Sir Robert's father executed in full view of both armies. The ensuing battle was a walkover for the Royal army as superior weaponry and training took its toll. The rebels fled and Sir Robert was eventually executed at Doncaster, along with his commanders. Bloody Oaks Wood by the A1 today is a reminder, and the nearby service station has the same name.

Greetham

S/F

PH   PH

Exton

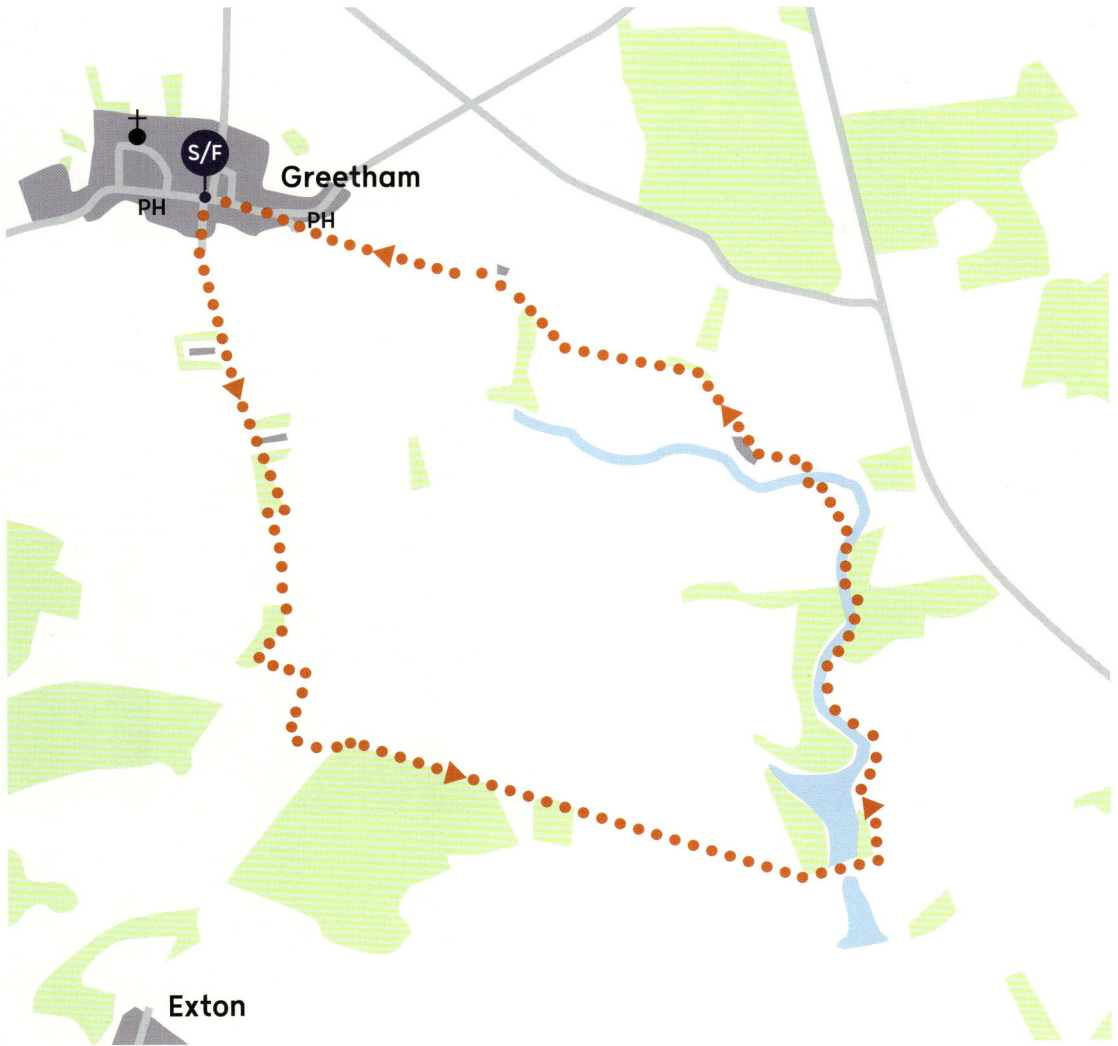

ESSENTIAL INFORMATION

Difficulty rating

🐾 🐾 🐾 ⚬ ⚬

Three paws; it's largely excellent underfoot, with no stiles, but can be muddy on the alternative option last stage back into Greetham. And it's more than five miles, so a proper two-hour walk.

Where to park
Anywhere responsible in Greetham.

Distance
Five and a half miles.

Highlights
Fort Henry and the absolutely straight mile on a peaceful estate road. This walk is also pretty good for winter because it's mostly on access roads. But beware it's exposed so wrap up warm if there's a cold wind.

Refreshments
The Wheatsheaf and The Plough in Greetham are both excellent. Or you can pop into the golf club or extend your walk into Exton and visit the Fox & Hounds.

The pooch perspective
You are unlikely to see any livestock on this route, but it is a conservation area with ground nesting birds, so control is vital. The North Brook offers the opportunity for fresh water.

West Deeping's Best Kept Secret

Set within 20 acres of beautiful grounds and waterways, Mr Molecey's Marvellous Mill is well worth knowing about.

Tim Steele

Situated on the road between Market Deeping and Stamford lies the stunning Grade II* listed watermill, now known as Molecey Estates. Glenn and Graham, the current owners, bought the Granary side of the property and its garden in 2015. They initially offered the Granary for house stays but soon the romance of the estate became apparent and the first wedding was hosted two years later. Since then Graham and Glenn have bought the adjoining Mill House and land and now the estate offers luxurious accommodation including 10 reception rooms and 15 themed bedrooms surrounded by gardens, rivers, streams and islands.

Glenn is joint owner of one of the oldest art galleries in London, Gladwell and Patterson, and Graham, who also works at the gallery, is a passionate historian and creative. Together they have produced the most stunning and unique setting. The house is a magnificent showcase of fine art and antiques, along with many treasures specifically sourced to relay the history of the great house and its ancestors. The surrounding tranquil gardens are bejewelled with an ever changing collection of magnificent sculptures, which are open to the public during 'Gallery in the Garden' in May and November.

Molecey Estates plays host to 10 or so weddings a year. Graham and Glenn, along with Little Glenn, prefer to keep to a smaller number so they can focus their attention on each couple and make sure each wedding weekend is as special and unforgettable as they imagined. The grounds are the perfect backdrop, adaptable to create either the romantic, the intimate or the daringly different celebration the couple are dreaming of. Over the years, strong relationships have been made with suppliers, celebrants, musicians and photographers so that couples can easily and reliably find the best fit for them.

As well as weddings, Molecey is offered for house stays - a very special home from home to spend time with family and friends and make long lasting memories together.

Cherrelle Blake

Molecey also accommodates corporate days and retreats, offering several unique event spaces alongside the grounds and house.

Graham and Glenn are active members of the local community, using local suppliers wherever possible for the house restoration and refurbishment, as well as for the weddings and also help to host community events such as the Deepings Literary Festival. The house and its landscape have truly been brought back to life, ready to be enjoyed and celebrated. With so much to offer it's hard to believe that you may not already know about Molecey Mill, but it really is marvellous.

HISTORY OF THE MILL

Molecey. Just one word. An unusual and very distinctive one. A family name, which is now, after centuries of use, firmly connected to one place - a magical and exciting out of this world setting.

Over the centuries Molecey was bustling with corn, mice, kingfishers, swans, flour sacks and carts. People arrived by canal from the coast. Stone and giant oaks were used to build the walls and floors.

Families came and went; in 1765 Jeremiah Sharpe inherited the mill. In 1772 it transferred to John and Eleanor Molecey who did lots of the building work including the Granary in 1773. Generations of their family lived here until in 1896 the Fullard family become the last in a line of 800 years of millers. The Rileys, with a famous artistic daughter, also called Molecey home from 1950 and the van Geests, through a successful banana business, secured its local fame over 30 years and brought the House, Mill and Granary safely through the twentieth century.

Sarah Carter

Cherrelle Blake

www.moleceyestates.com

Molecey Estate, Stamford Road, West Deeping, PE6 9JD

📞 07855 242356   📷 @moleceymill

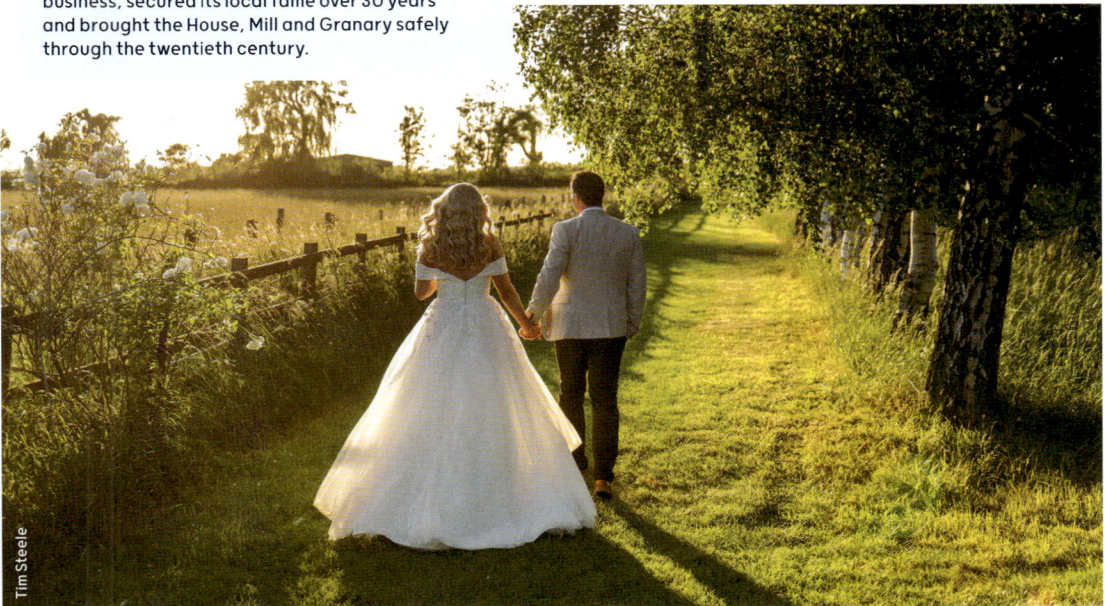

Tim Steele

Mr
MOLECEY'S
Marvellous Mill

9. Great Easton, Bringhurst and Nevill Holt

Idyllic and tiny Bringhurst and downright gorgeous Great Easton make this a good walk already, before you factor in Nevill Holt with its fascinating history and imposing hilltop location.

THE ROUTE

Park somewhere near the middle of Great Easton; one of the most attractive villages in the whole area. With a prominent church, decent pub and a plethora of stone-built thatched cottages it has a lot going for it. Not least some good walking. To start the route head west on Easton Road in the direction of Drayton and Medbourne but, as you near the western edge of the village, take the footpath signposted to the left into some grazing fields. This section is also part of the Jurassic Way which runs from Banbury to Stamford. Pass through a couple of grazing fields before entering a large arable field. As you get close to the far hedge take the obvious right branch in the footpath to head uphill towards Middleton Road which you will join just south of Bringhurst.

Walk up the hill on the tarmac in to almost Hollywood-pretty little Bringhurst. Yes, it does conjure images of *The Holiday* and you can almost imagine Cameron Diaz and Jude Law appearing in the doorway of one of the cottages here. Turn left to walk into the village and follow the road around the back of the church. Enjoy the gorgeous stone buildings, before going through a gateway and you will see a footpath post in the hedge on the right. Take the right-hand option here and leave the Jurassic Way behind.

> "You can almost imagine Cameron Diaz and Jude Law appearing in the doorway of one of the cottages here."

LOCAL KNOWLEDGE

Nevill Holt Hall is a Grade I
Listed building and dates to before
1300. It used to be a prep school
and is now owned by Carphone
Warehouse co-founder David Ross.
In the summer it hosts a festival
dedicated to opera, music, art
and literature.

It's downhill through a few small grazing fields over a stream and up into Drayton, which doesn't quite match the charm of some of the neighbouring villages. The footpath goes along the edge of a private garden and up the gravel driveway where you turn left and walk along the main road through the village for 200 metres or so.

Time to earn your rewards

Turn right on to Nevill Holt Road and leave the main drag behind. This is a quiet country lane and it is pretty much straight uphill for 600 metres, with most of the contours stacked into the last 100, so you will have really earned your magnificent view back to the south by the time you get to the left-hand turn at the top.

The footpath straight across the fields to Nevill Holt is clearly marked at this point and embraces a few more mini valleys on the way. By the time you reach the beautiful old hilltop hall your legs will know about it. Follow the path and stay on the eastern side of Nevill Holt until you can turn left and up into the hamlet. Turn right and left almost immediately on to Paddock Lane. Turn left again at the end and follow the road south along the western edge of the hall. You will see a footpath to the left which takes you back down along the magnificent ha-ha with views of the sculptures in the grounds. After the ha-ha, the path back

down the hill in a generally easterly direction towards Great Easton is fairly obvious.

Once you are on the path to Great Easton you will descend quickly away from Nevill Holt as you go through some arable fields initially, and then a series of smaller sheep grazing pastures. There is a small brook running along the northern edge of these fields with one or two access points for the dogs, which can be useful. Keep following the footpath signs and you will ultimately re-enter Great Easton on a little lane called Deepdale. There is a lovely fresh stream in the village so the dogs can cool off here too. Keep going on to Broadgate and then turn right on to the High Street and you can explore St Andrew's church and the rest of the village, before you arrive at The Sun for your refreshment.

Nevill Holt

Great Easton

S/F

PH

Drayton

Bringhurst

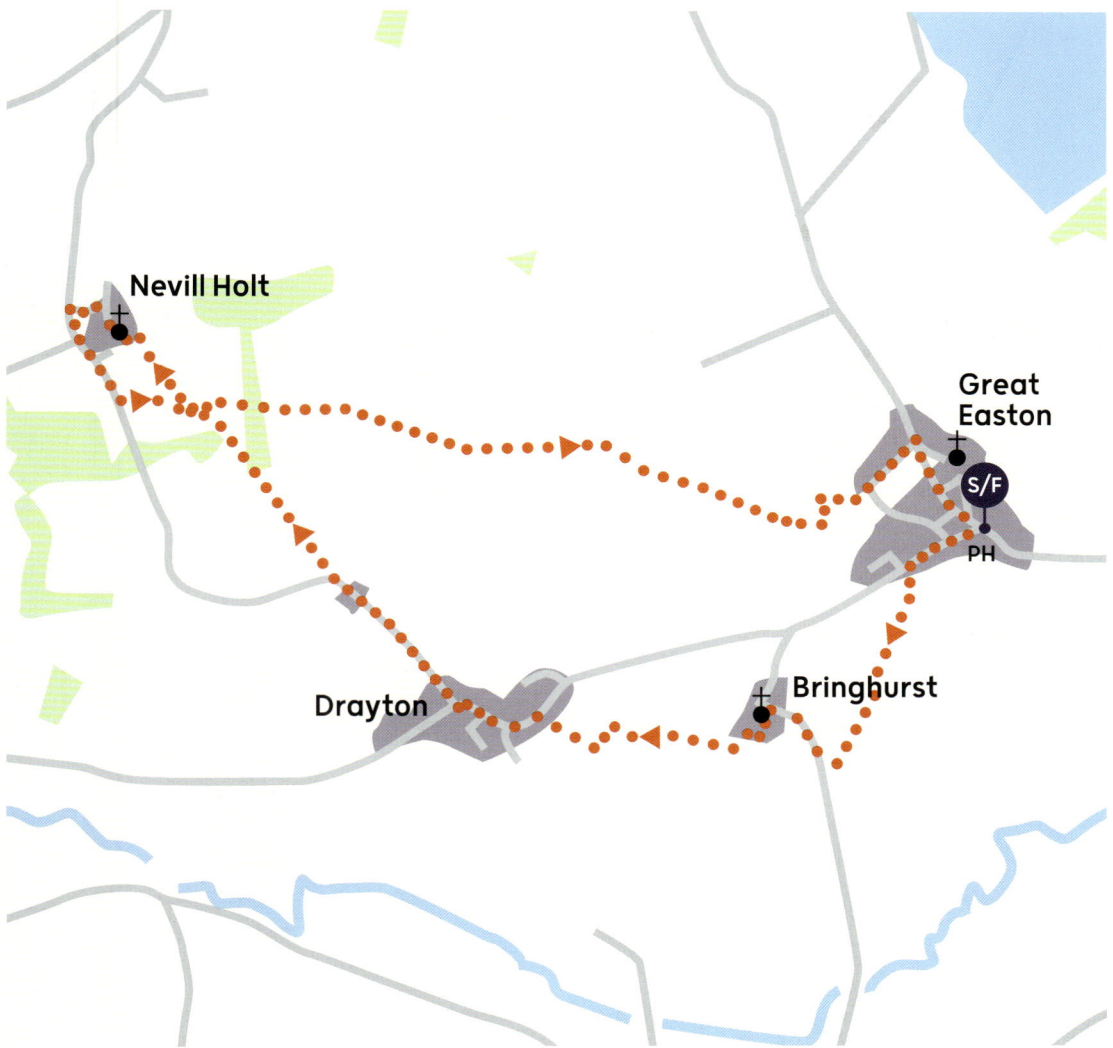

ESSENTIAL INFORMATION

Difficulty rating

🐾🐾🐾🐾🐾

Four paws. There are some quite steep sections and plenty of stiles.

Where to park
Anywhere responsible in Great Easton. I parked on Brook Lane.

Distance
Five and three quarter miles.

Highlights
Nevill Holt with its prominent position, sculptures and interesting history. Great Easton and Bringhurst are both as pretty as they come. Stunning views and a good pub.

Refreshments
The Sun in Great Easton.

The pooch perspective
With a lot of sheep you will have to keep the dogs on the lead for good sections of this walk, and there may be a shortage of fresh water in the hotter months.

10. Whissendine and Ashwell

Plenty of open country, a couple of railway crossings and a windmill all feature in this north west Rutland route.

THE ROUTE

You can park on the road near the White Lion down in the dip in the middle of Whissendine. Walk east away from the pub and pass the church on your left. After the right-hand turn in the road you will see the footpath sign on the left. Take this path and head out into some beautiful open countryside.

The path is well sign-posted for the next mile and a half as it arcs round to the south east through farmland and the odd piece of woodland. There are some lovely views on this stretch, and it really feels Far from the Madding Crowd.

Ultimately you will reach Whissendine Road just to the west of Ashwell. Turn left here and stay on the road to cross the Oakham to Melton railway line and walk into Ashwell. Turn right at the next junction and right again in a couple of minutes. You will then need to cross the railway again. When I last did this route the barrier was down, and I thought it might be stuck down but it came up eventually.

Mr MOLECEY'S
Marvellous Mill

> ❝
> Stay on the bridleway as it traverses the high ground here in north Rutland and enjoy the views in all directions.❞

Bridleway lottery

After the railway crossing, stay on Langham Road for nearly a kilometre as you go gradually uphill. When you reach the woodland at the top you will see the bridleway signposted to the right. The key word here is 'bridleway,' which unfortunately means when it has been very wet for a prolonged period the next stretch can be just about as muddy as it gets. It's fine in summer but be warned in winter – you will definitely need wellies and a sense of humour for a few minutes. It does get better though as the route goes on.

LOCAL KNOWLEDGE

Whissendine Windmill was built in 1809 and returned to milling in September 2006.

Stay on the bridleway as it traverses the high ground here in north Rutland and enjoy the views in all directions. After about one mile, you will see a route to the right which you could take to bring you back into Whissendine, but I recommend staying on the path for another ten minutes or so. Just as you are about to reach the road which connects Langham and Whissendine you will see a footpath to the right heading north.

Take this path through a few small fields initially and then follow it as it crosses a small stream. This is a peaceful little valley and after the stream crossing it's only another 10 or 15 minutes back into Whissendine where the excellent White Lion awaits.

Teigh

S/F
PH
Whissendine

Ashwell

Langham
PH

ESSENTIAL INFORMATION

Difficulty rating

🐾🐾🐾

Three paws; it's a well-marked route and is pretty straightforward, although if it's been very wet then the bridleway can become extremely hard work.

Where to park
On the main road in Whissendine between the White Lion and the church.

Distance
Six and a quarter miles.

Highlights
Some glorious open countryside and trees between Whissendine and Ashwell, plus a pretty little valley to finish. Also an excellent pub.

Refreshments
The White Lion in Whissendine.

The pooch perspective
You won't see a lot of livestock on this route as it's mostly arable land but be careful as always. There are a couple of streams on the way round.

MOLECEY'S
Marvellous Mill

11. Medbourne and Hallaton

This pretty corner of Leicestershire offers plenty of contours, two splendid villages with pubs to match, and a pilgrimage if you want to come back one day for a longer walk.

THE ROUTE

Park near the Nevill Arms in Medbourne and head north east out of the village on Uppingham Road, passing the church on the way. Once you have cleared the village and gone up a gentle incline you will see the path branching off from the road on the left in a northerly direction. It's a farm access road and offers great underfoot conditions as you pass through several fields. Look out for the left turn after approximately one mile just at some woodland on the left. Take this path and cross the stream to join the road between two cottages. Turn left and walk along the country lane for half a mile.

When you reach the T-junction you will see the footpath straight ahead. From here follow the signs and the path over a few stiles for nearly a mile until you come into Hallaton around the back of some houses. Turn left on to Eastgate and you will soon see the Bewicke Arms on the left. You have earned the right to a stop here if you have time. Otherwise, enjoy the grand buildings of this clearly prosperous old settlement which also hosts the famous bottle kicking match against Medbourne on Easter Monday every year. Once you have explored, look out for the left turn on to the footpath which leads south out of the village before you reach the church. It's almost a hidden doorway leading to the passage beyond.

LOCAL KNOWLEDGE

The 18-mile St. Morrell's Round is a pilgrimage around High Leicestershire which starts and finishes in Hallaton. It goes via Tugby, Loddington, Launde Abbey and Belton in Rutland and makes for a superb day's walking and inspecting the soul. I walked it on a cold and dry day in February and was blown away by the route. There is a museum at Hallaton where you can find out more: hallaton-museum.co.uk

This path leads on to Hare Pie Bank and the ancient site of St Morrell's chapel, which is now the basis of an 18-mile pilgrimage around the hills of High Leicestershire. That's not one for this walk, but I can assure you it's worth every step. There is an information board about the chapel on the five-bar gate and once you go through the gate turn left and follow the Macmillan Way down to Hallaton Road. Turn left and right again very shortly to stay on the Macmillan Way heading south. When you reach the next junction with Slawston Road you can turn left and walk straight back into Medbourne, but I prefer to carry on along Green Lane.

The lane cuts through the old dismantled railway line where there used to be a bridge, and shortly afterwards take the left turn on to the footpath at the field boundary. From here it's straight across the fields to Ashley Lane. Turn left and you will be in the Nevill Arms in five minutes. If it's winter you will be cosy inside and if it's warmer you can sit outside by the stream and watch the world go by.

> 66
> **Enjoy the grand buildings of this old settlement which hosts the bottle kicking match on Easter Monday."**

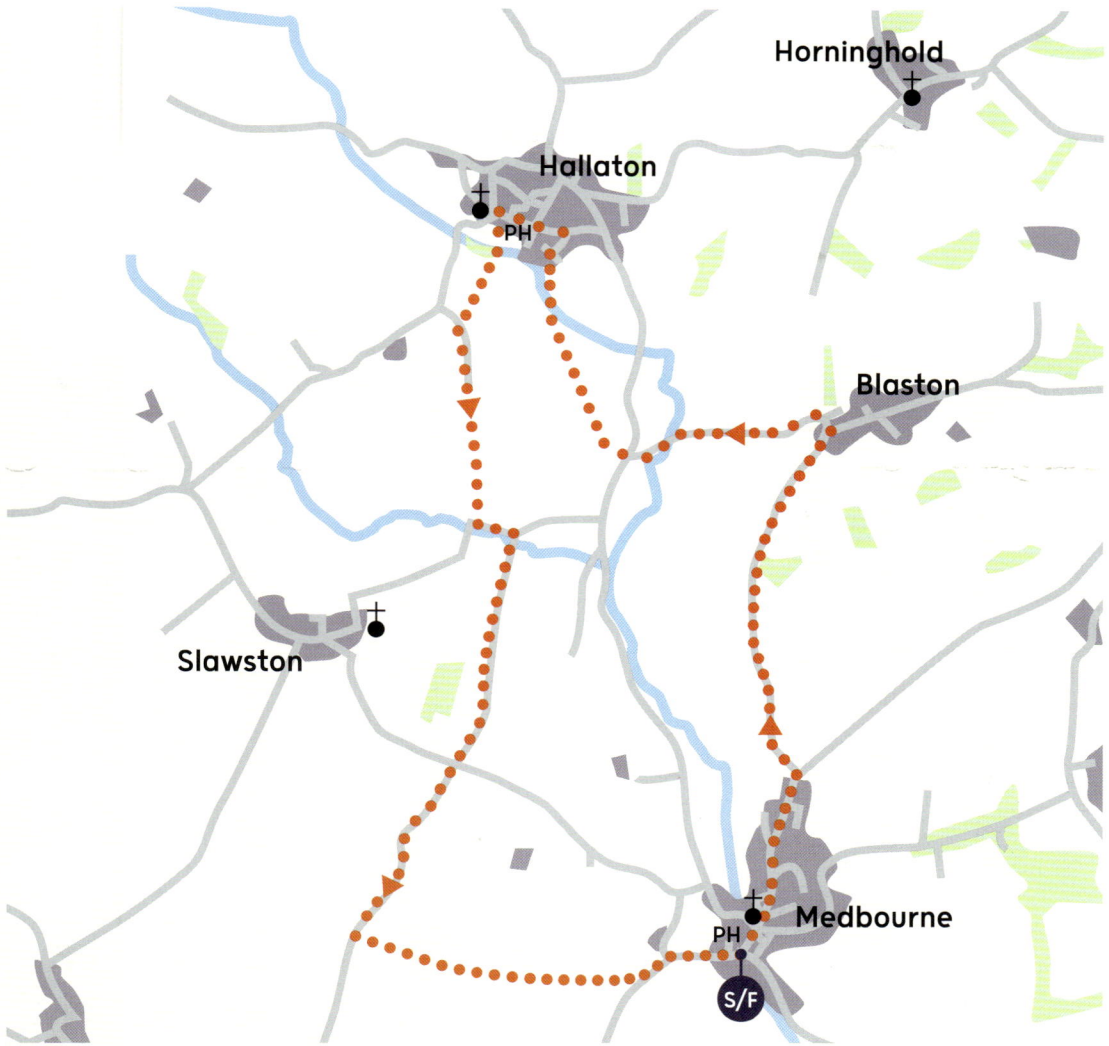

ESSENTIAL INFORMATION

Difficulty rating

😾😾😾😾🐾

Four paws. It's seven miles with some ups and downs and a few stiles.

Where to park
In Medbourne near the Nevill Arms.

Distance
Seven miles.

Highlights
The Nevill Arms is a landmark pub with rooms. Hallaton is surprisingly grand and the starting point of an 18-mile pilgrimage - St. Morrell's Round. The countryside is rolling but not spectacular.

Refreshments
The Nevill Arms in Medbourne and the Bewicke Arms in Hallaton.

The pooch perspective
You will probably encounter cattle and sheep at various points on the way round, but it's still a good leg-stretcher with the odd opportunity to cool off in a stream on a hot day.

12. Braunston-in-Rutland and Knossington

A serious walk with plenty of undulations in west Rutland and straying into Leicestershire.

THE ROUTE

Park somewhere near the Blue Ball pub and church in Braunston if you can. Enter the churchyard and walk around to the western end where you will see the path before you. Head out into the farmland beyond and ignore the first left to keep bearing west. When you come to a small stream (the very early Gwash) after about half a mile make sure you take the left-hand option after crossing, otherwise you will go up to the road with nowhere to walk but tarmac.

From here keep heading south west for another mile. The path goes through South Lodge farm and then crosses over the stream before coming to a four-way junction with a bridleway running north/south. Cross over the bridleway and take the path which heads slightly north west on the opposite side. Stay on this path until you reach a country lane. Turn right here and head uphill on the road for about 500 metres until you get to the T-junction.

You will see the footpath sign straight ahead so proceed through the gate and follow the path through pastureland and then on to a track as you pass Preston Lodge down to your left. Take the first left hand turn after Preston Lodge to head downhill and over the stream. From here the path heads north over farmland for more than a mile on the way to Knossington. It's remote, rural land and makes for peaceful walking.

66

You are now back in Rutland and just about to pass the highest point in the county (197m)"

Hilltop village

You will arrive in the splendid hilltop settlement of Knossington via the Manor House on your left. Turn right on to the road and if you want to visit the Fox & Hounds for light refreshment turn left at the next junction and follow the road around. The pub has a nice patio at the front and a beer garden behind but is not always open on weekday afternoons. If you want to skip the pub, turn right at the junction and walk along Main Street and then on to The Hollow. Go down through the dip and as you start heading uphill you will see the gates to a large house on the right in the trees and a footpath sign. Turn right here to enter the grounds of Bleak House and then follow the footpath signs as they guide you out into the open country. There are plenty of undulations here and your legs will start to feel it.

After Bleak House the path goes east through several sheep grazing fields on the way to the field before Lady Wood Lodge, where it can be hard to see the path and the exit. Head to the north east corner of the field and enter the farmyard. Keep heading east and you will see a footpath sign or two on the side of the farm buildings as you pass through to confirm you are on the right track.

Stay on the path as it leaves the farm behind and then skirts along the bottom edge of Cold Overton Park Wood. You are now back in Rutland and just about to pass the highest point in the county (197m) to your left. There is a trig point here but it's not actually on the footpath. Five minutes after the end of the wood you will come to a junction at the fence, where you will enjoy some fine views over Rutland Water and much of the county. Turn right here on to the bridleway and then left in approximately 500 metres on to another bridleway. Follow the signs and you will come to a right turn in the hedgerow. From here it's one kilometre downhill all the way back into Braunston where the Blue Ball awaits.

LOCAL KNOWLEDGE

Nearby Launde Abbey is a stunning Elizabethan Manor House built on the site of an Augustinian Priory. It is now used as a retreat and for conferences and weddings, but also has an excellent café.

ESSENTIAL INFORMATION

Difficulty rating

🐾 🐾 🐾 🐾 🐾

Five paws; it's quite a long way with a lot of contours and a few tricky stiles.

Where to park
Somewhere in the middle of Braunston near the church.

Distance
Seven and a quarter miles.

Highlights
This is a proper walk with many undulations and your legs will know about it. A lot of it is over remote and peaceful farmland, but both Braunston and Knossington are attractive villages.

Refreshments
The Blue Ball in Braunston and the Fox & Hounds in Knossington (not always open during the day).

The pooch perspective
You will see a lot of sheep on this walk, and some cattle. There are streams every now and again and places without livestock but be warned, you will see sheep and cows.

13. Barrowden, Harringworth, Seaton and Morcott

This fabulous route in the Welland valley includes four villages, two pubs, an idyllic village green, a viaduct and a meandering river.

THE ROUTE

Barrowden is one of the prettiest villages in Rutland, with a striking village green, duck pond, and a pub overlooking the whole idyllic scene. You can park anywhere responsible around the green, or on one of the roads nearby. Starting from the Exeter Arms, head west along Main Street and branch left on to Seaton Road. Almost immediately turn left on to a wide driveway and take the footpath over a stile to the right. From here follow the path south-west for a mile towards the Welland, with a few turns along the way, and lovely views to Northamptonshire across the border to the south. Cross the river at Turtle Bridge and turn right immediately to follow the meandering waterway westwards.

MOLECEY'S
Marvellous Mill

LOCAL KNOWLEDGE

The viaduct is a striking feature of this walk. It was completed in 1878, is more than a kilometre long and 30 million bricks were used to build it. At one point 3,500 men and 120 horses were employed in the construction, and Cyprus Camp on the north side had 47 huts and a population of 560 people. It remains an incredible example of Victorian engineering and construction.

In approximately one kilometre you will arrive in pretty Harringworth, lying in the shadow of the mighty 82-arch railway viaduct which spans the valley here. Head west out of the village on Gretton Road and, 50 yards before you reach the viaduct, take the path to the right across the field and underneath the arches. Follow the path as it recrosses the Welland and goes around Seaton Mill. Cross the road at the end of the drive and head uphill through sheep pastures to Seaton. From its hillside perch this little village offers superb views of the valley and viaduct. It also has an excellent pub, the George and Dragon, which can be hard to walk past.

Whether the pub draws you in or not, the route continues east out of the village on Main Street. Immediately after the pub go straight on at the crossroads and stay on this wonderful country lane for a kilometre as it drops downhill. There is an alternative path to Morcott

to the left as the road bends right, but for this walk I suggest staying on the road downhill over the old railway bridge to the T-junction, where you turn left. After 200 more metres on the tarmac take the left turn on to the bridleway. When you get have climbed a little on this bridleway make sure to turn around and appreciate the view down to the viaduct and beyond.

At the end of the bridleway, you will then rejoin the road down to Morcott for 500 metres. Cross the busy A47 with care, and walk along the A6121 for 100 metres. Turn right on to the footpath which skirts around the back of the village and means you don't have to walk along the busy main road. Recross the A47 and then pick up hedge-lined Morcott Road all the way back into Barrowden, passing the Morcott windmill near the start. When you get back to Barrowden, the Exeter Arms will be waiting for you.

> 66
> **When you have climbed a little on this bridleway turn around and appreciate the view down to the viaduct."**

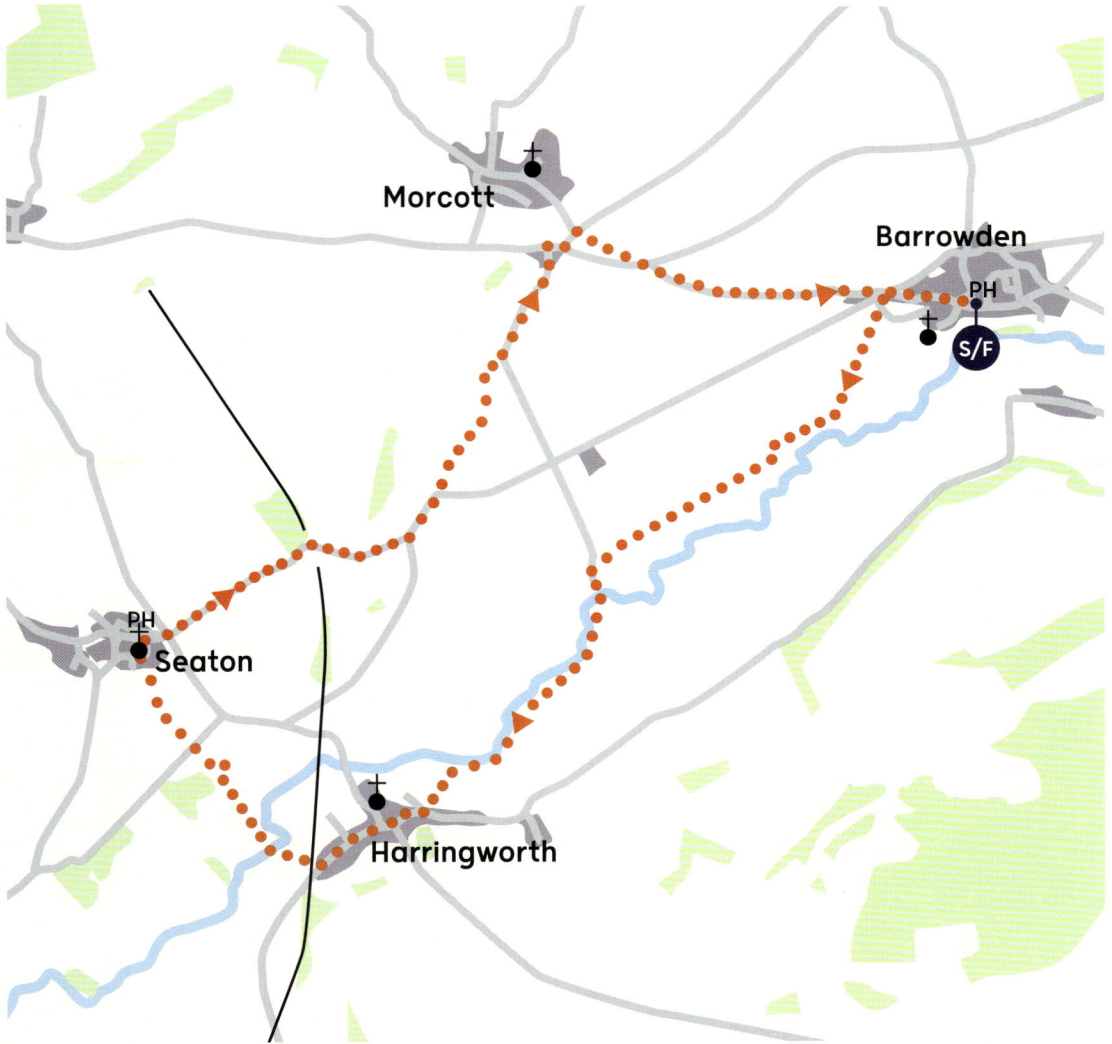

Morcott

Barrowden

PH

S/F

Seaton

PH

Harringworth

ESSENTIAL INFORMATION

Difficulty rating

🐾🐾🐾🐾🐾

Four paws; there are quite a lot of stiles and some of them are tricky, plus it's more than seven miles with a few hills.

Where to park
Somehere near the Exeter Arms in the middle of the village.

Distance
Seven and a half miles.

Highlights
Pretty villages, a viaduct, the river, lovely views and two good pubs.

Refreshments
The Exeter Arms in Barrowden or the George and Dragon in Seaton.

The pooch perspective
Good in terms of dipping in the river in the first half, but be warned you will see plenty of sheep so take care

"
You will soon come to your first encounter with the Chater where there is a good spot for the dogs."

14. The Luffenhams, Pilton, Lyndon and Wing

With five villages in a peaceful part of Rutland, this is a great option for a weekend expedition.

THE ROUTE

Park near the church in North Luffenham and in the corner where Chapel Lane meets Digby Drive you will see a small iron gate in a stone arch which is your gateway to this wonderful walk. From here, head downhill through a couple of green fields, until the path brings you out on the road where you turn right. You will soon come to your first encounter with the Chater where there is a good spot for the dogs to get in if they want. After the river go under the railway and up the hill and turn left at the junction to head towards South Luffenham.

On arrival in the village look out for the bridleway on the right just after you pass the junction with Cutting Lane. Take this turn and head gradually uphill across an arable field. The route is then enclosed by hedgerows for a stretch before crossing the road between Morcott and North Luffenham. Stay on the path as it gradually wends north west towards Pilton and joins the road on a bend 300 metres from the village. Walk into quiet and almost unheard-of little Pilton and turn right at the junction. Follow the road past the church and, shortly after passing the last house on the right, you will see the footpath leaving the road on the left on a bend. Take this path and follow it westwards for more than a kilometre until you reach the Wing to Lyndon road. Cross the road and follow the path across the last fields before Wing.

The heart of Rutland

When you get into the village you can walk along the main street and turn right down Middle Street. Turn right at the bottom and you will see the footpath on the left almost immediately. Take this path and head downhill along the hedge on the right-hand side. Turn right at the bottom and then cross the railway after a short distance. Follow the footpath and you will come to a bridge over the Chater – another handy spot for the dogs to cool off and have a drink.

After you cross the bridge turn right and head north east back across the hillside towards Lyndon via a series of right angle turns. Follow the signs and you will cross a bridge over a small stream in a narrow stretch of woodland before approaching Lyndon along the south side of grand old Lyndon Hall, which was completed in 1677.

When you reach the road at the end of this path just by a grand red brick house on your left, take a moment to appreciate the tree-lined avenue running downhill to your right before turning left to resume the walk. Turn right at the next junction and leave Lyndon via Picks Barn café, a place with a great reputation.

After Lyndon it's a mile and half on the road all the way back to North Luffenham, but with magnificent trees creating a cathedral like canopy overhead and hardly any traffic you won't begrudge the time on the tarmac. And when you reach North Luffenham The Fox pub will be waiting to soothe your aching limbs with a pint of whatever you desire.

LOCAL KNOWLEDGE

In 1642 North Luffenham was the scene of a minor siege in the English Civil War. Royalist Henry Noel knew that Lord Grey and his parliamentary forces were on the rampage nearby so retreated to his house, Luffenham Hall, with a defensive body of men. Lord Grey and his 1,300 soldiers surrounded the Hall but there was little actual fighting, and outnumbered Noel had little choice but to surrender.

Edith Weston

Lyndon

North Luffenham

PH

S/F

Pilton

PH
Wing

South Luffenham

PH

PH

Morcott

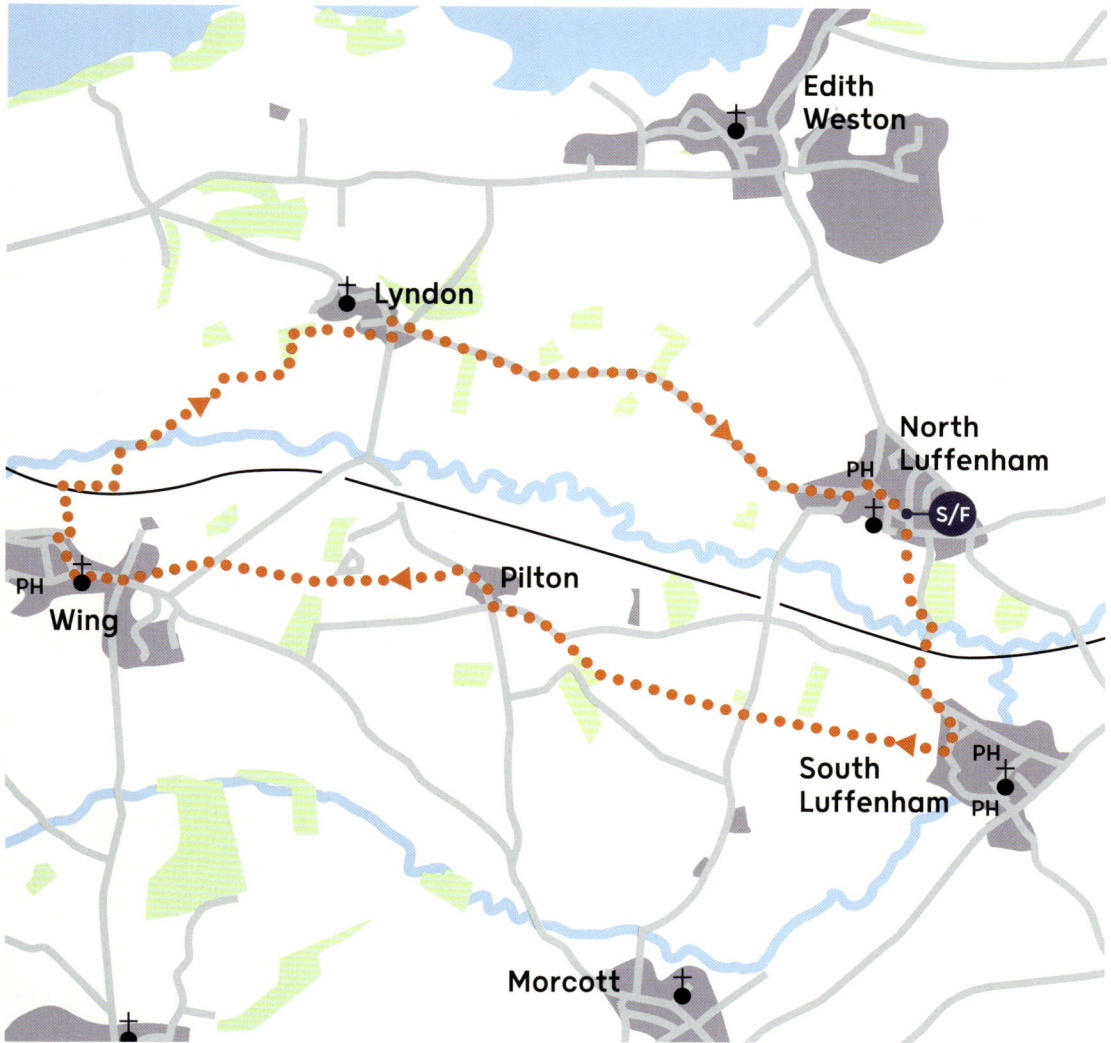

ESSENTIAL INFORMATION

Difficulty rating

🐾🐾🐾

Three paws; at more than seven miles it's a proper walk, but a lot of it is very good underfoot and there aren't many tricky stiles.

Where to park
In North Luffenham near the church.

Distance
Seven and a half miles.

Highlights
A peaceful valley with a series of quiet and attractive villages, Lyndon Hall, tree-lined roads and very little traffic.

Refreshments
Picks Barn in Lyndon, The Fox in North Luffenham and two pubs in South Luffenham if you make a detour.

The pooch perspective
Two opportunities to cool down in the Chater and largely arable, although you will probably see some livestock and there's at least two miles on the tarmac.

Mr
MOLECEY'S
Marvellous Mill

15. Uffington, Greatford and Barholm

Two of the area's best pubs make this long walk worth every step.

THE ROUTE

Park in Uffington and head west along the main A1175 past the church and Greatford Road. After you pass the layby on the right and just before the final row of houses take the footpath to the right just before a bungalow.

Follow the path north out on to the fields on a track with good views of Stamford down to the left. After approximately one mile turn left and follow the path west on the farm track initially, and then along the edge of two fields, passing Cobbs Nook Farm on your left until you reach the junction in the tree-lined bridleway. Turn right on to the bridleway and stay on the path for nearly a mile. If it's berry season you may be in for a treat. When you reach Essendine Road at the end of the bridleway turn left and then turn right at the junction. Stay on the road all the way to the railway crossing. If the barriers are down when you get there make sure you get across swiftly when they go up.

After the crossing stay on the road for the next half a mile until you reach the footpath on the left which heads into Shillingthorpe Park. Take this path and walk down the tree-lined avenue and cross the bridge over the West Glen river. Head uphill on the track, enter the woods at the gate and, after one more minute, take the right-hand path through the gate. Follow this path across the fields and towards Greatford. You will come in on the path behind Greatford Hall and through Greatford Gardens. Turn right on to the road through the village, cross the pretty bridge, and then turn right at the T-junction in the middle of the village. The path to Barholm is on your left almost immediately (just before the Hare & Hounds) and it goes through a farmyard before heading into the fields beyond. Follow the path and cross the bridge over the Greatford Cut drainage channel.

A welcome break

"
Take this path and walk
down the tree-lined avenue
to the West Glen river."

You will shortly come into Barholm behind the church over a couple of old stone stiles. Turn right at the road and head straight to the Five Horseshoes (not open till 4pm on weekdays) where you will be able to take a well-earned rest, having already completed the lion's share of the walk. If it's warm weather the expansive terrace and garden will offer you plenty of space, and in the colder months of the year there are few cosier places in the area than the inside of this wonderful old pub.

Once you have rested sufficiently walk out of the pub car park and turn left. Follow the road as it bends round and becomes a lane. Cross the stile at the end of the lane and follow the path ahead, across another stile, over the next field and then along the edge of two large fields. When you get to the end of the wood on your left, cross another stile and head to the gate by the East Coast mainline. Take extreme care when crossing the railway here. Trains can be travelling in excess of 100mph, but

you have a clear view for a long way in both directions.

Once you have crossed the railway follow the signs and the path as it crosses two fields in a south westerly direction. After the second larger field go through the gateway into the Casewick Hall area. Follow the road past some lovely houses before going through another gateway and passing Casewick Hall on your left. It's three separate residences these days but retains its original visual splendour and is an under-rated place of calm and beauty with a ha-ha and large lawn.

Follow the road out of Casewick Park through the grand old gates and keep going until you reach the outskirts of Uffington. Look out for the footpath on the left which will take you round past the playground and into the welcoming world of the Bertie Arms. Here you can rest your weary legs and quench your thirst.

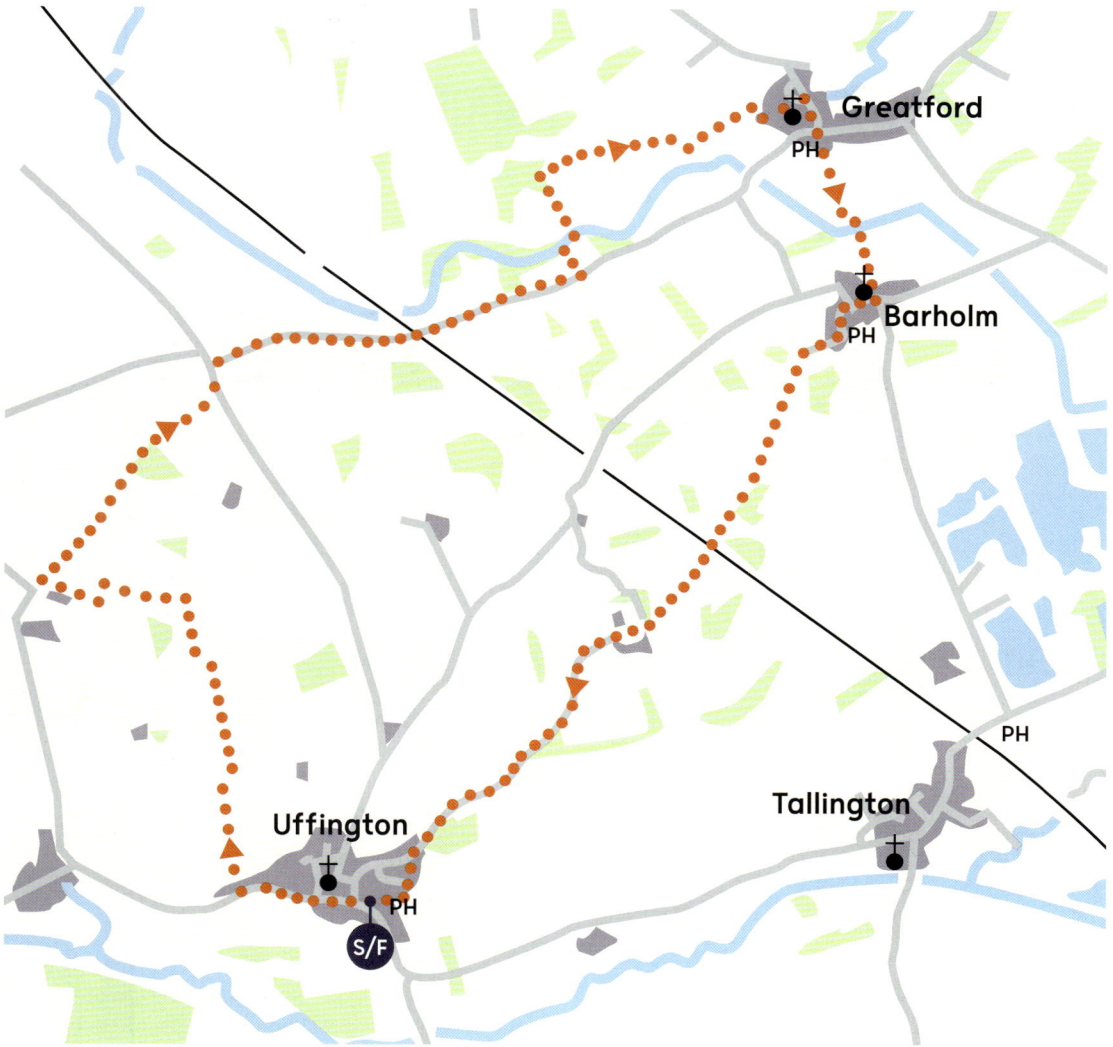

ESSENTIAL INFORMATION

Difficulty rating

🐾🐾🐾🐾🐾

Five paws; it's pretty easy going underfoot all the way round but it's more than nine miles and there are some awkward stiles around Barholm.

Where to park
Somewhere responsible near the Bertie Arms in Uffington.

Distance
Nine and a quarter miles.

Highlights
Plenty of open countryside, the mile-long bridleway to Essendine Road, Shillingthorpe Park, Casewick Hall and Park and two superb village pubs.

Refreshments
The Five Horseshoes in Barholm (not open till 4pm on weekdays) and the Bertie Arms in Uffington.

The pooch perspective
The dogs will absolutely love this walk in plenty of arable fields. The West Glen river and the Greatford Cut both offer an opportunity for a paddle.

How to be a happy walker

Some guidelines for staying safe and enjoying your walking.

Navigation

All the routes in this guide are along rights of way but please take a map or download the OS App because you never know when you might need it. Make sure you know the route before you start and look out for the signs. They are generally pretty good but sometimes they go missing…

Sheep & dogs

There are lots of them so please make sure you close the gates behind you and keep your dogs on a lead whenever you see sheep or a sign asking you to do so. And on the subject of dogs, please make sure you clean up after your beloved canine.

Parking

Please park considerately in villages. Don't block driveways, entrances or narrow roads. If it means walking a few more metres to get to the start point then that's just some more steps for you.

Footwear

Wear what is comfortable for you but remember it can get very muddy indeed in the winter, so trainers may not work in January. Although in the summer months a lot of these routes are like walking on tarmac.

Provisions

It's always sensible to take some water and a few snacks. We tend to get grumpy when thirsty and hungry. And check the weather forecast before you head out. A waterproof is often a useful addition.

Be a good patron

If you are visiting any of the pubs in this guide please be careful if you have muddy boots (clean or remove them before entry), and ask if dogs are welcome. All the pubs in this book were in operation at the time of going to press, but it's a difficult economic climate in the hospitality industry, so use them or lose them. Remember, pub car parks are for customers only, and just in case you are wondering, we have not partnered with any of the pubs mentioned - they feature because we like them.

> **66**
>
> Make sure you know the route before you start and look out for the signs. They are generally pretty good but sometimes they go missing…"